THE WRITER'S BOOK OF SYNONYMS

CORPORATION
THE WRITE TRACK COMPANY

Gail Gompper
Illustrator

Dr. Nolan Estes
Educational Consultant

A NOTE TO THE TEACHER

THE WRITER'S BOOK OF SYNONYMS will serve two important purposes in helping your students write.

  . It can be used as a handy word-reference guide.
  . It will extend and enrich written vocabulary.

By using **THE WRITER'S BOOK OF SYNONYMS** frequently, your students will learn many new words and if they use the dictionary along with this book, they will become aware of different shades of meaning.

The student must also understand that **synonyms** are words that are **similar**, but **not the same**, and are used only when they clarify the meaning of text or improve the style. This understanding, of course, comes gradually with maturation and experience.

The entry words in this book have been selected from the basic written vocabulary of students. For example, the student might use the word **strong** and need to know different synonyms. By looking up the word **strong**, the student will find **dauntless, tenacious, unintimidated,** and others.

In addition to synonyms, this book contains lists of classified nouns. Under the heading **HOW ANIMALS ARE NAMED**, the student will find, for example, an entry titled **fish family**. Under this entry are listed shark, bluefish, tuna, barracuda, piranha, and others. Some of the names will be known to most of the students; others will be recognized only by those who have a special interest in this form of animal life.

You will find that the synonyms under each entry are arranged randomly rather than in order of difficulty. We have used this arrangement to encourage the students to review all the words before making a choice. Students who have their own copy of the book can also add their own synonyms.

We believe that your students can improve their writing by using the enlarged vocabulary which this book provides and we hope that you find **THE WRITER'S BOOK OF SYNONYMS** to be a useful addition to your writing program.

HOW TO USE THIS BOOK

This book is designed to help you locate words when you are writing. It will help you find exact words for your sentences. Sometimes one word works better than another.

Read the following sentences:

The elephant walked through the jungle.

The elephant stomped through the jungle.

Which sentence helps you see a picture in your mind of how the elephant moved? The second sentence - **The elephant stomped through the jungle.** - helps you imagine the elephant's movement more clearly. When you write, you must help your reader imagine the scene that you are creating with words.

At the beginning of the book there is **THE WORD LOCATOR CHART** which contains three categories: **PEOPLE, ANIMALS, AND THINGS.** Suppose you need a word to describe the sounds a dog makes.

First, look in the **WORD LOCATOR CHART** which begins on page 1 and find the category **ANIMALS.**

Second, find the subhead **How Animals Communicate.** This heading will be listed alphabetically using the C in **Communicate** as the key word.

Third, under that subheading find **Dog Family.** This too will be listed alphabetically using the **D** in **Dog** as the key word.

Fourth, find the page number. On that page you will find a list of words that describes how dogs and members of the dog family such as wolves and coyotes communicate. Choose the word that best describes what you want to write about. Following each group of words is an example sentence using one of the words in the group.

For example, if you want your dog to sound angry, your sentence might read:

The **dog snarled at the man.**

If you want to have your dog sound happy, you might write the following:

The dog yapped loudly at **his master.** We have labeled each word group **NOUNS, VERBS,** or **ADJECTIVES.** The nouns will be the names of items that belong to the same category. They may not necessarily be synonyms. For example, **rattlesnake** and **alligator** are not synonyms, but both are reptiles.

Keep in mind that many synonyms do not have exactly the same meaning. Each word has its own "shade of meaning". If you are not sure of the shade of meaning, use your dictionary to help you decide which word from the **WORD GROUP** is the best to use.

Use your synonym book every time you write. It will make learning how to use similar words easy and will make your writing more interesting.

WORD LOCATOR CHART

PEOPLE

How People **Act**

How People **Communicate**

How People **Do Things**

How People **Look**

THINGS

SYNONYM LIST

PEOPLE

How People Act

excited (adjectives)

spirited	stirred up	inspired
aroused	animated	agitated
gingery	peppery	stimulated
provoked	thrilled	fired up
spunky		

Example: The **spunky** girl refused to accept defeat.

foolish (adjectives)

stupid	fat-headed	dense
half-witted	dull	dunce-like
unintelligent	brainless	moronic
dumb	witless	

Example: The **witless** boys poked sticks at the copperhead snake.

happy (adjectives)

joyful	glad	jolly
cheerful	ecstatic	pleased
delighted	merry	content
gleeful	lighthearted	jovial
blissful	satisfied	

Example: The tennis player leaped over the net, **delighted** over her victory.

mean (adjectives)

nasty	villainous	malicious
disagreeable	intolerable	vicious
foul	ugly	coarse
rude	gross	despicable
vile	vulgar	indelicate

Example: The **malicious** people threw stones at the house.

nice (adjectives)

pleasant	friendly	charming
likeable	pleasing	agreeable
gracious	good	cultured
kind	tasteful	

Example: The **friendly** children volunteered to help the senior citizens plant a vegetable garden.

sad (adjectives)

unhappy	dispirited	dissatisfied
sorrowful	grieving	discouraged
mournful	depressed	dejected
discontented	apathetic	displeased
disheartened		

Example: The baseball player was **depressed** by his inability to hit a home run all season.

shy (adjectives)

bashful	timid	diffident
quiet	reserved	wary
retiring	cautious	timorous

Example: The boy was too **bashful** to ask the beautiful girl to dance.

smart (adjectives)

wise	talented	resourceful
alert	bright	adroit
ingenious	astute	quick-witted
clever	keen	intelligent
brilliant	masterly	
sharp	artful	

Example: The chess player's **brilliant** move won the game.

strong (adjectives)

tough	dauntless	heroic
forceful	gallant	tenacious
daring	bold	unintimidated
unafraid	undaunted	

Example: The knights of medieval times were **gallant** fighters.

talkative (adjectives)

long-winded	wordy	rambling
chatty	garrulous	gossipy
loquacious	gabby	verbose

Example: The **long-winded** speaker ruined the debate.

tired (adjectives)

worn	weary	listless
drained	spiritless	fatigued
weak	exhausted	sluggish

Example: The **weary** plowman plodded home after an exhausting day.

tireless (adjectives)

energetic	unflagging	unwearying
untiring	unfailing	indefatigable
vigorous	spirited	strenuous

Example: Eleanor Rossevelt was **vigorous** in her efforts to achieve world peace.

weak (adjectives)

frail	decrepit	intimidated
debilitated	feeble	cowardly

Example: The ninety year old man is too
feeble to feed himself.

afraid (adjectives)

frightened	cowardly	alarmed
timorous	scared	terrified

browbeaten

Example: The **terrified** parents called the
police at 4 A.M. to report their
daughter missing.

How People **Communicate**

cry (verbs)

moan	whimper	snivel
wail	lament	sob
bewail	weep	bemoan
blubber	shed tears	groan

Example: The man **sobbed** for hours when
his dog did not come home.

laugh (verbs)

roar	chortle	snigger
cackle	giggle	howl
chuckle	snicker	shriek

Example: The three witches **cackled** over their brew.

scream (verbs)

yell	holler	bellow
cheer	squeal	whine
shriek	shout	screech
howl		

Example: Mr. Smith **bellowed** at the boy and frightened him out of his wits.

sing (verbs)

hum	chant	serenade
warble	wail	intone
moan	carol	croon

Example: "Let's go **caroling** with our neighbors on Christmas day," the children suggested.

smile (verbs)

grin	beam	smirk
simper	snicker	

Example: The father **beamed** delightedly when his daughter received the award for best athlete.

talk (verbs)

chat	babble	speak
utter	confer	discuss
slur	argue	gab
spout	whisper	converse
mumble	sputter	rattle

Example: The teacher **spoke** sharply to her class.

write (verbs)

scribble	trace	enter
author	print	imprint
autograph	process	stamp
pen	impress	mark
type	compose	sign

Example: Herman Melville **authored** many books, including <u>Moby Dick</u>.

How People Do Things

attack (verbs)

fight	rush	battle
storm	besiege	assail
destroy	ambush	overrun
waylay	assault	mug
strike	bombard	charge

Example: The enemy **bombarded** our homes and factories.

carry (verbs)

haul	bear	hold
transfer	support	move
transport	convey	transmit

Example: The girl **transported** the logs from the forest to her farm.

dance (verbs)

disco	jig	shimmy
polka	flutter	waltz
prance	sway	shuffle
glide	stomp	tap

Example: As the couple **glided** across the dance floor, they heard the applause from the audience.

drive (verbs)

transport	propel	roar
fly	truck	haul
speed	bus	race
chauffeur		

Example: The boy **roared** around town in his car.

eat (verbs)

bite	munch	digest
gulp	wolf-down	gobble
devour	gobble-up	gnaw
chew	feast	consume

Example: The young hikers **devoured** their lunch.

exercise (verbs)

stretch	jump	push
practice	bend	crouch
drill	leap	kick
lift	squat	jump
exert	develop	train

Example: Lifting weights **develops** strong muscles.

fight (verbs)

box	bicker	squabble
clash	skirmish	scuffle
spar	brawl	contest
wrestle		

Example: **Bickering** over money causes much unhappiness.

help (verbs)

assist	champion	back
support	aid	relieve
defend	uphold	

Example: The arrival of the Prussians **relieved** the hard-pressed British army at Waterloo.

jump (verbs)

skip	romp	bound
spring	leap	parachute
somersault	hurdle	vault

Example: The girls **skipped** past my window.

lift (verbs)

load	elevate	pick up
heave	boost	raise
hoist		

Example: The workmen **elevated** the platform up to the second floor.

run (verbs)

dash	scramble	jog
sweep	lope	hurry
flee	shot	scamper
pace	race	dart
blot	trot	sprint
rush	spring	scurry
glide	wing	

Example: The people **scrambled** onto the bus.

walk (verbs)

stomp	stride	plod
parade	swagger	tramp
trek	hike	stroll
meander	promenade	saunter
march	amble	waddle

Example: **Strolling** through old neighborhoods is a pleasant activity for many people.

fat (adjectives)

chubby	stout	portly
pudgy	puffy	blubbery
stocky	beefy	round
obese	plump	fleshy
heavy	sturdy	thickset

Example: The **portly** man waddled down the street.

old (adjectives)

aged	ripe	antique
decrepit	elderly	hoary
ancient	infirm	

Example: We often forget to honor our **aged** heroes.

pretty (adjectives)

beautiful	delicate	fair
dainty	comely	proportioned
lovely	bonnie	

Example: In Scotland, a **bonnie** lass means a pretty girl.

short (adjectives)

tiny	undersized	petite
dwarfed	slight	pint-sized
minute	teeny	runty
modest	wee	puny

Example: Although the woman was **slight** of build, she carried a heavy package.

skinny (adjectives)

thin	lanky	gaunt
emaciated	slight	lean
frail	slender	scrawny
slim	wiry	drawn

Example: Actors in horror movies often have a **gaunt** look.

strong (adjectives)

muscular	sinewy	well-built
powerful	stalwart	sturdy
robust	athletic	stout
brawny	husky	

Example: The **brawny** wrestler pounded his chest and grinned at the audience.

tall (adjectives)

| lofty | gawky | towering |
| statuesque | lanky | stringy |

Example: The **towering** basketball player was able to touch the basketball hoop with his hand.

ugly (adjectives)

homely	loathsome	hideous
repulsive	beastly	disgusting
unsightly	grotesque	

Example: "Get out of my house, you **loathsome** thief," shouted the elderly man.

weak (adjectives)

puny	gaunt	decrepit
spare	infirm	feeble
impotent	slight	fragile
frail		

Example: The **puny** boy knew he was no match for the powerful bear.

young (adjectives)

junior	girlish	boyish
youthsome	juvenile	maidenly
youthful	babyish	

Example: Even though the man was nearly
sixty years old, he retained
a **boyish** smile.

How People Are **Named**

boy (nouns)

youth	laddie	youngster
guy	stripling	prince
male	lad	kid
schoolboy	chap	fellow

Example: The **youth** cried when he lost his
wallet.

crook (nouns)

gangster	hoodlum	scoundrel
criminal	villain	thief
felon	knave	mobster
rascal	robber	rogue
bandit	swindler	

Example: The **robber** cautiously opened the
window and stealthily
entered the house.

girl (nouns)

maiden	lass	tomboy
female	schoolgirl	miss
lassie	damsel	princess

Example: Marsha hated being called a **tomboy.**

hero (nouns)

champion	winner	protector
defender	victor	

Example: As the fans wildly cheered, Chris knew she was the new **champion.**

man

sir	male	gentleman
Mr.		

Example: "What is your name, **sir**?" inquired the lad.

woman (nouns)

lady	Ms.	Mrs.
female	feminist	

Example: The **feminist** fought for equal rights for all people.

classify (verbs)

arrange	organize	categorize
systematize	sort	catalog
group	analyze	file
coordinate		

Example: Scientists have **grouped** animals according to their common characteristics.

concentrate (verbs)

analyze	focus	scrutinize
meditate	weigh	study
explore	dwell upon	examine
contemplate		

Example: The biologists carefully **scrutinized** the bacteria under the microscope.

guess (verbs)

wonder	surmise	assume
infer	suspect	muse
presume	theorize	imagine
conjecture		

Example: "I **presume** she wants the job," **mused** the boss.

imagine (verbs)

dream	conjure	fancy
picture	visualize	envision
create	muse	conceive

conjecture

Example: Martin Luther King **envisioned** a
world of peace and racial harmony.

plan (verbs)

design	outline	concoct
engineer	plot	scheme
frame	organize	diagram

Example: Scientists can **design** rockets
to travel faster than sound.

reason (verbs)

examine	calculate	weigh
consider	mull over	study
ponder	infer	deliberate
muse	estimate	cerebrate
judge	concentrate	

Example: The student **pondered** over the three
possible answers before making
a decision as to which one might
be correct.

remember (verbs)

recall	reminisce	review
meditate	recollect	re-examine
rethink	reflect	

Example: The old man **reflected** upon all the wonderful things he had done as a youth.

study (verbs)

examine	deliberate	cogitate
survey	ponder	observe
contemplate	consider	dissect
investigate	research	

Example: The child carefully **examined** the tiny insect under a microscope.

suppose (verbs)

suspect	deduce	assume
hypothesize	presume	conjecture
dream	speculate	

Example: Everyone **assumed** that the old woman was unfriendly because she never left her house.

ANIMALS

How Animals Act

angry (adjectives)

wild	frenzied	fierce
enraged	rabid	ferocious
untamed	mad	

Example: The **fierce** lion crouched in the bushes waiting to attack the small animal.

frightened (adjectives)

scared	terrified	cowed
threatened	startled	disturbed
alarmed		

Example: The **startled** animal retreated into shadows.

happy (adjective)

frolicsome	high-spirited	frisky
lively	springy	playful

Example: "You certainly are **frisky** today," said the man as his dog bounded off the chair.

How Animals **Communicate**

bird family (verbs)

sing	trill	twitter
tweet	chirrup	coo
warble	peep	pipe
chirp	caw	troll

Example: The meadowlark **piped** a happy tune.

cat family (verbs)

meow	cry	shriek
roar	growl	snarl
purr		

Example: The giant panther **snarled** at the intruder.

dog family (verbs)

snarl	howl	bay
yelp	wail	cry
bark		

Example: The coyotes **wailed** in the moonlit desert night.

How Animals **Look**

appealing (adjectives)

cuddly	soft	graceful
tiny	sinewy	fuzzy
attractive	fluffy	sleek

Example: The **sleek** deer bounded over the fence.

big (adjectives)

huge	elephantine	ungainly
gigantic	clumsy	giant
stupendous	mammoth	enormous
large	immense	powerful

Example: Many authors write charming stories about the **ungainly** hippopotamus.

fierce (adjectives)

wild	enraged	infuriated
threatening	frenzied	menacing
crazed	ferocious	ravenous
savage	mad	

Example: The **frenzied** animal attacked its enemy.

little (adjectives)

small	teeny-weeny	teeny
petite	wee	slight
tiny	diminutive	undersized

Example: Sitting on a huge stump was the most **diminutive** chipmunk I had ever seen.

How Animals **Move**

bird family (verbs)

fly	swoop	loom
whisk	float	whiz
hover	flutter	soar
glide	flap	plunge

Example: The eagle **plunged** from its mountain perch towards the water.

cat family (verbs)

slide	stoop	scud
crawl	slink	leap
crouch	glide	spring
stalk	pounce	scuttle
scamper		

Example: The tiger **glided** quietly through the tall bush.

deer family (verbs)

vault	jump	scoot
bound	scud	spring
skip	leap	scurry
bounce		

Example: As the moose **vaulted** over the
fallen tree, the hunter took aim.

dog family (verbs)

crawl	frisk	crouch
spring	prowl	heel
leap	pounce	attack
jump	scoot	

Example: The hungry dogs **prowled** for food
in the dark, unfriendly forest.

fish family (verbs)

swim	skim	propel
scurry	scoot	float
dart	glide	dive
flutter	leap	

Example: **Swimming** near the surface of the
water, the school of bluefish made
a beautiful sight.

horse family (verbs)

jump	pace	lope
race	canter	gallop
spring	trot	pound
leap		

Example: Gallant Hero **pounded** down the track ahead of all the other horses in the show.

large animals (verbs)

trot	stamp	plod
charge	thud	stomp
lope	thunder	clump
gallop	sway	lumber
jump	waddle	

Example: Fleeing from ivory hunters, the elephant herd **thundered** across the plains.

reptiles (verbs)

slip	glide	scamper
curl	crawl	twist
slither	leap	spring
slide	coil	swim

Example: The tiny lizard **scampered** across the path.

How Animals Are **Named**

bird family (nouns)

albatross	cuckoo	parrot
blackbird	dove	pelican
bluebird	eagle	penguin
bluejay	finch	pigeon
buzzard	gooney bird	raven
canary	hawk	roadrunner
cardinal	hummingbird	robin
crane	oriole	seagull
crow	parakeet	

Example: The huge **crane** balanced itself on
one leg.

cat family (nouns)

Abyssinian	leopard	panther
alley cat	lion	Persian
bobcat	lynx	puma
cougar	Manx	Siamese
Himalayan	mountain lion	tiger
jaguar	ocelot	wildcat
kitten		

Example: The giant **cougar** waited patiently
on the overhanging limb.

deer family (nouns)

black-tailed deer moose   reindeer

caribou   mule deer   white-tailed deer

elk

Example: **Caribou** are used for food and clothing by people in the far north.

dog family (nouns)

Beagle	Fox	Poodle
Bloodhound	Foxhound	Schnauzer
Bulldog	Great Dane	Scotch Terrier
Chihuahua	Greyhound	Sheep-Dog
Cocker Spaniel	Hound	Shepherd
Collie	Husky	St. Bernard
Coyote	Irish Setter	Terrier
Dalmatian	Jackal	Wolf
Dingo	Pekingese	

Example: It is hard to believe that the **Chihuahua** and the **Great Dane** belong to the same family.

fish family (nouns)

barracuda	flounder	sailfish
bass	fluke	salmon
blackfish	mackeral	sawfish
bluefish	perch	sunfish
bonita	pike	swordfish
carp	piranha	trout
catfish	porgy	tuna
eel	ray	weakfish

AND

sharks (great white, blue, mako, tiger, hammerhead, sand, pygmy, thresher, basking, whale shark)

Example: Catching a **barracuda** is very different from catching a **flounder**.

large animals (nouns)

bear	dinosaur	hippopotamus
bison	donkey	orangutan
buffalo	elephant	rhinocerous
bull	giraffe	steer
camel	gorilla	zebra
cow	horse	

Example: **Gorillas** and **orangutans** belong to the primate family of animals.

reptile family (nouns)

adder	cobra	painted turtle
alligator	coral snake	rattlesnake
anaconda	copperhead	sea turtle
blacksnake	crocodile	snapping turtle
boa constrictor	garter snake	tortoise
box turtle	Gila monster	water moccasin (also cottonmouth)
caiman	iguana	
chameleon	lizard	

Example: A reptile that changes its colors is called the **chameleon.**

water mammals (nouns)

dolphin	porpoise	sea lion
manatee	seal	walrus

whale (pilot, sperm, white, humpback, finback, blue, killer whale)

Example: **Dolphins, porpoises,** and **seals** are very playful animals.

THINGS

How Things **Feel**

glue, gum, putty

gooey	sticky	gummy
pasty	soft	pliable

Example: The wallpaper was **gooey** after we smeared on the glue.

grease, oil

silky	smooth	slick
tacky	slippery	slimy

Example: The water felt **slimy** after the oil spill.

earth (adjectives)

round	jagged	rocky
bumpy	pebbly	rugged
gritty	stony	coarse
soft	hard	

Example: The **soft** earth oozed between our toes.

mud (adjectives)

boggy	slimy	soft
mucky	sludgy	slippery

Example: The **soft, slimy, slippery** mud bogged us down.

sand (adjectives)

hot	cool	pebbly
smooth	gravely	coarse
grainy		

Example: Sand from beneath the ocean is dark and **coarse.**

cold (adjectives)

freezing	nippy	frigid
brisk	bone-chilling	chilly
icy		

Example: The **brisk** weather kept many people from the picnic.

heat (adjectives)

sultry	simmering	sweltering
parching	scorching	oppressive
smothering	blazing	blistering

Example: The **blistering** heat made many people feel weak and fatigued.

rain (adjectives)

drizzly	wet	soggy
cool	driving	misty
damp	bone-chilling	

Example: My skin was stung by the **driving** rain.

snow (adjectives)

wet	cold	frozen
crisp	icy	chilly
fluffy	sloshy	slushy

Example: The **fluffy** snow melted as it
touched our warm hands.

How Things Look

buildings (adjectives)

tall	gigantic	soaring
lofty	towering	sturdy
enormous	glass-covered	

Example: **Glass-covered** buildings look very
modern.

deserts (adjectives)

dry	deserted	bleak
rainless	golden	thirsty
arid	empty	barren
bare	sandy	desolate

Example: Stretching endlessly before the
weary patrol was the **bleak** desert.

fire (adjectives)

red	flashing	roaring
flaming	raging	gleaming
shimmering	blazing	glimmering
glowing		

Example: The **raging** fire destroyed the walls of the barn.

heavenly bodies (adjectives)

gleaming	glowing	shimmering
flickering	twinkling	flashing
dazzling	beaming	glittering
blazing	glaring	radiant
sparkling		

Example: Ranging across the night sky are millions of **glittering** stars.

houses (adjectives)

a. **haunted houses**

frightening	spooky	ghostly
horrid	horrible	creepy
ghastly	evil	terrifying
horrifying	menacing-looking	

Example: Outlined against the moon stood the **terrifying ghostly** house.

b. mansions

kingly	queenly	grand
splendid	glorious	dignified
elegant	majestic	lordly
regal	stately	

Example: The **stately** mansion was fit for a royal family.

c. old houses

deserted	aged	abandoned
deteriorating	decayed	worn
crumbling	withering	weathered

Example: I returned to my old neighborhood and was saddened by the **abandoned** houses on every street.

knives/nails/swords (adjectives)

sharp	sharp-edged	barbed
angular	needle-sharp	keen
tapered	pointed	toothed
jagged	razor-edged	sharp-toothed

Example: The swordsman flashed his **sharp-toothed** dagger through the air.

smoke (adjectives)

dark	gray	grimy
white	drifting	billowing
wafting	blackened	blinding
black	choking	

Example: The **dark** smoke billowed from the burning lumber.

water (adjectives)

a. calm water

blue	green	clear
sparkling	still	glistening
shimmering	tranquil	placid

Example: The **placid** ocean resembled a lake.

b. rough water

stormy	wild	angry
gray	violent	crashing
fierce	choppy	turbulent
agitated	rushing	roaring

Example: After six days of rain, the **turbulent** waters broke through the dam.

weather (adjectives)

a. rainy day

cloudy	dark	dim
misty	gloomy	dismal

Example: The continuous rain assured us
of a **dismal** day.

b. snowy day

glowing	bright	peaceful
glistening	shimmering	dazzling

Example: I was dazzled by the **glistening** snow
which looked like a field of
diamonds.

c. sunny day

bright	clear	radiant
golden	sparking	

Example: The **golden** days of summer end too
soon.

40

How Things **Move**

airplanes/clouds/gliders/kites (verbs)

dive	sail	drop
drift	climb	glide
whisk	take off	loop
lift	skate	roll
spin	coast	roar
stream		

Example: The giant jet **climbed** high above the clouds.

baseballs/tennis balls/basketballs (verbs)

bounce	rebound	flip
whiz	toss	swish
soar	shoot	arch
fly	ricochet	fire

Example: The basketball **arched** through the air.

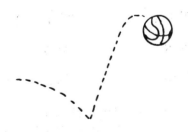

bicycles/tricycles/unicycles (verbs)

roll	turn	wheel
bounce	pedal	lurch
spin	brake	

Example: The bicycle **braked** swiftly to a stop.

buses/cars/motorcycles/trucks (verbs)

whiz	breeze by	slide
roll	careen	crawl
screech	speed	creep
spin	race	buck
roar	rev	veer
jerk		

Example: The huge car **careened** around the corner.

grass/leaves/trees (verbs)

flutter	reach	rock
swing	whip	rustle
bend	sway	quiver
lean	flap	stir

Example: The tall grass **whipped** back and forth in the wind.

swings/treetops/vines (verbs)

dangle	rock	oscillate
swoop	sweep	swing
sway		

Example: Hundreds of vines **dangled** loosely
from the trees.

water/wind (verbs)

crash	sweep	splash
shake	rage	lap
roar	swirl	

Example: The waves **raged** against the rocks
reminding us of their anger.

How Things Are **Named**

buildings (nouns)

skyscraper	stadium	sports arena
capitol	tower	monument
structure	edifice	brownstone

Example: The **skyscraper** reached towards the
clouds.

fights (nouns)

battle	clash	war
feud	conflict	brawl
squabble	combat	attack
quarrel	scuffle	

Example: The British **attack** on Baltimore in 1812 lasted far into the night.

flowers (nouns)

blossoms	boutonniere	floret
floweret	posy	corsage
bud	bouquet	

Example: Apple **blossoms** are often associated with weddings.

forests (nouns)

woods	woodlands	timberland
grove	thicket	jungle

Example: The cry of wild animals echoed throughout the **jungle**.

hats (nouns)

cap	high hat	fez
turban	beret	helmet
lid	hood	sombrero
tam	derby	Panama
bonnet	ten-gallon hat	fedora
crown		

Example: Today most hockey players wear **helmets**.

houses (nouns)

cabin	mansion	split-level
castle	habitation	tent
igloo	adobe	shelter
shack	ranch	bungalow
hogan	palace	lean-to
hut		

Example: The pioneers built **log cabins** in the wilderness.

mountains (nouns)

cliff	range	butte
mount	ridge	alp
chain	upland	plateau
peak	sierra	mesa

Example: The Spanish word for a flat mountain is **mesa**, which means table.

pain (nouns)

ache	twinge	stitch
spasm	seizure	throbbing
crick	soreness	pang
pinch		

Example: The **throbbing** in her head would not go away.

rain (nouns)

drizzle	monsoon	downpour
cloud-burst	shower	mist
sprinkle	deluge	precipitation
hail		

Example: The **mist** spread across the lonely valley.

sleep (nouns)

nap   doze   snooze

slumber   dream   catnap

siesta   rest   hibernation

Example: The child had a **dream** about
          Christmas trees and presents.

snow (nouns)

slush   hail (stones)   flurry

blizzard   snowfall   precipitation

sleet

Example: The **hailstones** were the size of golf
          balls.

How Things **Smell**

attics/cellars (adjectives)

damp   rank   moldy

rancid   moist   musty

stale   clammy

Example: There was a **moldy** smell coming
          from the cellar.

flowers (adjectives)

lovely	refreshing	sweet
fresh	perfumed	fragrant
redolent	aromatic	sweet-smelling
pleasing		

Example: A **refreshing** smell of gardenias filled the entire room.

garbage dumps/sewers (adjectives)

foul	rank	rancid
reeking	musty	putrid
offensive		

Example: The **putrid** odor of rotting garbage was everywhere.

hospitals/medical buildings/doctors' offices (adjectives)

clean	fresh	sanitized
scrubbed	disinfected	antiseptic
sterilized		

Example: I woke up after the accident and recognized the **antiseptic** smell of a hospital.

oceans/seas/bays (adjectives)

salty	briny	marshy
fishy		

Example: The **marshy** air announced that the
sea was nearby.

How Things **Sound**

bells/glass (verbs)

ring	bong	gong
jingle	resound	ding-dong
toll	peal	chime
clamor	ding	clink
clang	tinkle	

Example: The bells of the church **chimed**
the good news.

books/clothing/paper (verbs)

flip	crinkle	wave
rustle	ruffle	swish
stir	snap	blow
flap	ripple	undulate

Example: Old Glory **waved** proudly over Fort
McHenry.

coins/hammers/metals (verbs)

jingle	chime	thump
clatter	ring	bang
clink	clap	clank
clang	rattle	jangle

Example: As the train **clattered** into the
the empty station, the father
kissed his teary daughter farewell.

earthquakes/thunderstorms/volcanoes (verbs)

roar	crack	thunder
blast	wail	explode
rage	burst	erupt
boom	crumble	howl

Example: The black storm clouds **thundered**
out of the east.

watches/clocks (verbs)

tick	click	jangle
chime	jingle	tap
ring out	beat	stroke
tick-tock	boom out	

Example: In the darkest hour of the night, the
tower clock **boomed out** its
melancholy sound.

How Things Taste

cakes/candy/sweets (adjectives)

sweet	honeyed	mouth-watering
delicious	rich	luscious
sugary		

Example: The **mouth-watering** pastries on the waiter's cart tempted me to break my diet.

grapefruit/lemons (adjectives)

sour	pungent	biting
acrid	sharp	tart
bitter		

Example: The **tart** tast of lemon goes well with fish.

ice cream/milk/yogurt (adjectives)

cold	refreshing	rich
fruity	icy	creamy
thick	milky	smooth
frosty		

Example: This **fruity** yogurt is imported from France.

soda (adjectives)

fizzy	bubbly	sweet
sugary	icy	refreshing
cold	sparkling	

Example: **Sugary** soda and good dental health do not go together.